A Godly Prune

May each "cut" lead to
clusters of sweeter fruit -
fruit that remains.

Mary H. Blake

MHB Publishing Company
Georgia, USA

www.mhbpublishingcompany.com

M H B
PUBLISHING
COMPANY

Scripture quotations taken from the Holy Bible, New International
Version (NIV), New Living Translation (NLT), and New American Standard
Bible (NASB).

Printed in the United States of America.

ISBN: 9798999659927

Dedication

To the One who prunes with love—
Thank You, Lord, for every cut that draws me closer to You.
To my family—my beloved husband, children, and grandson—
Your love, support, and prayers have been a steady vine in every season.
And to every reader—
May this book meet you in your pruning and lead you into lasting fruit.

With all my heart,

Mary H. Blake

Table Of
Contents

Dedication

01	Introduction
02	Opening Prayer
04	Ready To Be Pruned
06	Godly Pruning
12	The Levels of Pruning
16	Stages of Pruning
22	Signs of Pruning
28	Types of Pruning
44	Journaling Prompts
49	Growth
56	Prayers that Seal

Introduction

"Pruning moments" are seasons or experiences in your life where God lovingly removes something to help you grow just like a gardener cuts back healthy branches so a plant can bear more fruit (John 15:2). They may feel painful or confusing at first, but they're not punishment they're **preparation for greater purpose, fruitfulness, and closeness with God**.

Hebrews 12:10-11. 10 *For they disciplined us for a short time based on what seemed good to them, but he does it for our benefit, so that we can share his holiness. 11 No discipline seems enjoyable at the time, but painful. Later on, however, it yields the peaceful fruit of righteousness to those who have been trained by it.*

Let's be Clear: *There are many levels of pruning, but they are all different, they overlap, repeat, and look different for each believer. Pruning is more repeated than you think, it is much like actual vines that are trimmed every season.*

Let us start with prayer, we want to make sure that our heart is open and ready to be pruned. The pruning is not just about pain, but it's for purpose. It allows for God to make over our character, strengthen us, develop us for His Will and purpose.

Opening Prayer

Father, The gardener of my soul, I come before You with open hands and a tender heart.
Your Word says that you prune every fruitful branch so it can bear even more fruit (John 15:2).

Lord, I yield to your pruning, and I align with your word. Let your Holy Spirit take everything out of me that does not align with your will for my life. I submit to the leading of your spirit and confess to the power of your Word. Discipline is always for my good, that I can share in Your holiness. Lord, in this cutting season I feel the sting and the need to confess that I need to change. Lord, I do not always recognize what you are shaping in me or why you have removed certain leaves and blossoms from my Life. Reveal your will for my life. I rest in your pruning for I desire more of you. Lord, have your way in my life.

Father, prune me until my life tastes like Christ, sweet, nourishing, and enduring. May every cut becomes a conduit for greater love, deeper holiness, and wider influence for Your kingdom. I trust Your hands. Finish what You have started and let it all be for Your glory.

In Jesus Name

Amen.

Are You Ready to Be Pruned?

These are the questions every growing believer must face.

The context of these questions are for you to:

- Not to be punished, but to be **prepared and be a better version of who God see.**
- Not to lose, but to become **lighter** in your heart, knowing that it is working for your good.
- Not to impress people, but to *abide* tightly with God, Jesus and the Holy Spirit.

The gardener is ready. Are you ready?

1. Are you ready to let God touch the places you've kept hidden?
2. Are you ready to give up what feels fruitful—but isn't faithful?
3. Are you ready to release good things, so He can give you God things?
4. Are you ready to stop striving and start surrendering?
5. Are you ready to trust His shears more than your own plans?

Remember:
Being pruned doesn't mean you're failing. It means you're **fruitful enough to be refined.**

Encouragement

Embrace it, if God is pruning you, it means you're already connected to Him and producing fruit. He simply wants you to grow even more. In my life, I have seen many moments of pruning. Let me tell you, it can really mess with your mind if you think it's all about what you did, rather than who He wants you to become. Life has its way of trying to bully you, problem after problem and storm after storm. It may seem as if God is punishing you for something. If you're not careful, you begin to pray like, "Lord I am sorry for whatever I did, please make it stop!". Yes, I have prayed those prayers, too.

But God, had to teach me that life is a lesson, and only God has the ability to turn a mess into a message. As you go through the stages of pruning, get you out of the way, and look for God's loving hand to lead, guide and direct you.

I had to learn through God instructing me that sometimes; Godly pruning doesn't always make sense in the moment. God sees the branches that are using up energy and space in your life, but they are not producing real fruit. God wants the things we don't show on the outside. The things that only you and God knows. Often, the deepest pruning happens in the heart: pride, unforgiveness, insecurity, and hidden idols. So, embrace the pruning, embrace the things that God reveals and the level of pruning you go through in order to be better. If you're asking, "What do I have to do to be better?" You don't just need self-improvement. We need to surrender. We need to be better, spiritually, emotionally, or even practically.

Hebrews 12:6
"He disciplines those He loves..."

5

Godly Pruning

Set the Scene:

Before you begin to read, sit quietly for a minute. Picture a vineyard at dawn—vines recently pruned, dew on the fresh-cut branches. Ask the Holy Spirit to cultivate expectancy in your heart.

Anchor Passage

Slowly read **John 15:1–17**, concentrating on verse 16.
You did not choose me, but I chose you. I appointed you to go and produce fruit and that your fruit should remain, so that whatever you ask the Father in my name, He will give you.

Read it twice, then say it aloud, letting each phrase settle in your heart. _____

Companion Scriptures

* **Galatians 5:22-23** *(the fruit of the Spirit). Are you having trouble with living up to any of these attributes? Your cutting may start there.*
* **Hebrews 12:11** *No discipline seems pleasant... but later it produces*
* **Isaiah 55:10-11** *God's word always bears fruit.*

_____

Reflect & Journal
  1. Identify the Cuts
What recent "pruning" moments (losses, corrections, inner convictions, shift in commitments, relationship shifts...etc.) can you name?

_____

_____

_____

2. How did it feel at first?
What were your emotions? (confusion, sadness, grief, discomfort, pain, inadequate...etc.)

_____

_____

_____

3. Spot the Fruit (Gal 5:22-23)
Which fruit of the Spirit seems to be the ripest during this season of your life?

_____

_____

_____

4. Fruit That Remains
Imagine five years from now. Which outcome of today's pruning could still bless others?

Write a sentence beginning with:

"Because God trimmed_____,

I can now _____

_____

_____

_____

Encouragement

When God reveals something in your heart that needs to be removed like an attitude change, fear, worry, motive, hidden sin, you must know that it is not a moment of shame. It's a moment of *invitation*. God is inviting you to open up your heart in order to remove what should not be so that we can trust God in all things.

It's ***Godly Exposure***. He is not exposing you to condemn. He is revealing to **heal**, *to* **cleanse**, *to* **refine**, *and to* **make room** *for new* **fruit**.

I can recall, a time in my life I was going through something very troubling. It was consuming me. It began to shift my thoughts and how I began to view things.

I cried out to God in prayer, but prayer was not enough. Yes, you heard me, prayer was not enough. It was not until I allowed God to open up my heart. God revealed to me that my heart was sick and full of fear, worry, anxiety, and doubt. That thing broke me. I thought to myself, how could I love God so much, serve him completely and yet carry so much within my heart.

God simply gave me a gentle whisper; "Daughter, It's in your heart". My spirit broke before God. I began to cry out to God to show me where my fear and worry was coming from! He led me right to his word.

Psalm 139:23-24
23 Search me, O God, and know my heart;
Try me and know my anxieties; 24 And see if there is any wicked way in me, and lead me in the way everlasting.

Psalm 73:26
26 My flesh and my heart fail;
But God is the [a]strength of my heart and my portion forever.

God had to see what was in my heart, God had revealed that my heart was in pain. Pain can be a silent killer. I was holding onto past struggles, past fears. I began to trust what was in my heart as a final answer. Rather than trust in God and His word.

God showed me that you cannot trust even the things in your heart unless God's presence is visible, we must have an active appetite for God's word, or the devil will deceive you. He comes to make you think you are *ok* and *all is well*.

Meanwhile, you are walking through life, without hope, without complete trust in God and His will. Your views, your responses, your attitude begin to lean to your own understanding. Trusting in your own way and mind, distorts God's truth. For this is the reason why you can't trust what's in your heart, without knowing that it's being fully led by the Holy Spirit and God's word.

Jeremiah 17:9
"The heart is deceitful above all things, and [a]desperately wicked. Who can know it?

Yes, deceit in the heart will lead you away from the will and word of God if you let it. Deceit is described as, "**the action or practice of deceiving someone by concealing or misrepresenting the truth**." Deceit can be in the form of many things, dishonesty, deceptive, crafty, misleading, untruthful, and many other distorted truths.

God says in His word, that we can trust in a heart that is submitted to Him. When we allow God to create in us a clean heart and renew us with His Word. You can rest in the words of the Lord and find peace.

Ezekiel 11:19-20

19 Then I will give them one heart, and I will put a new spirit within [a]them, and take the stony heart out of their flesh, and give them a heart of flesh, so that they may walk in My statutes and keep My judgments and do them; and they shall be My people, and I will be their God.

This is another aspect of pruning, allowing God to take out of you, the thing that doesn't belong in your heart. This brings about a heart that can fully trust in the Lord.

Proverbs 3:5-7

5 Trust in the Lord with all your heart, and lean not on your own understanding;
6 In all your ways acknowledge Him, and He shall [a]direct your paths.
7 Do not be wise in your own eyes; Fear the Lord and depart from evil.

Remember:

In your pruning season, your heart posture can reveal many things to us. It can reveal a heart that is bitter, unforgiveness, pride, self-righteousness, envy, jealousy, or comparison and even control issues and so much more. We have to remain open to the Spirit of God and allow his word to lead and guide us daily.

The Levels of Pruning

The Levels of Pruning:

So, there are levels of pruning in God, we are not all at the same level. We are not all going through the same level of pruning at the same time. There are times in your life that God must prune you for distinct reasons. Many believers find that God's "pruning" comes in progressive layers or levels, each one designed to draw us into deeper fruitfulness and intimacy with Him. Scripture does not give a numbered list of stages, but it does show that God's pruning can range from gentle shaping to more radical cutting back, all with the goal of greater growth.

Pruning Levels

Level of Pruning	What it often looks like	Key Scriptures	Fruit God is after
Surface Trimming	Conviction over obvious sins or habits that hinder witness (language, honesty, media choices).	John 15:2a; 1 John 1:9	Visible obedience, cleaner witness
Habit-Reshaping	Restructuring time, priorities, and relationships—He prunes distractions, "good" things that crowd out the best.	Eph 5:15-17; Heb 12:1	Consistency, disciplined life (Prayer, Word)
Heart-Motives	The Spirit exposes pride, people-pleasing, hidden idols. Circumstances force us to surrender control.	Ps 139:23-24; Prov 4:23	Purity of motive, humility, single-minded devotion
Character-Refining	Trials that test faith, reshape temperament (impatience, anger, fear). Often prolonged seasons.	Jas 1:2-4; Rom 5:3-5	Perseverance, maturity, Christlike character
Mission-Focusing	God removes even fruitful branches that aren't part of *your* calling, redirecting gifts or location. Costly obedience.	Acts 16:6-10; Jn 15:2b	Maximum kingdom impact, focused stewardship
Deep Surrender	Dark night" moments: reputation, comfort, or long-held dreams are laid down. He becomes enough.	Phil 3:7-10; Heb 12:11	Intimacy, unshakeable joy, multiplied fruit

Encouragement

Seasons are a real thing! I can recall a time in my life when my children were small, and someone gave me a book by the Lois Evans, "Seasons of a Woman's Life". I did read the book, but it was not until later that I began to live out the various seasons of my life. I went back to this book, and it helped me to remember that seasons change. We all will face a changing season for sure, it's part of God's natural pruning.

Life got a little hectic for me, raising young children, being a young pastor's wife, being a sister, daughter, friend and so much to many others. But with all of this going on, God was still requiring me to allow Him to garden my life.

Removing unproductive branches, unfruitful habits and facing difficult life circumstances. These seasons taught me how to commit to the things of God. Letting go of control and trusting God's plan even when things were hard and uncomfortable.

While seasons shift and change. God's faithfulness and love will remain throughout every life season and change. Just as pruning will be a seasonal shift and change. You will find that in this season; God is actively removing off the things both good and bad in order to grow us into spiritual beings for His kingdom.

Pruning is a process where God is refining us and revealing to us, all at the same time. He refines who he called us to be, and He reveals to us who He is to us. You will see this scripture in John, throughout this book. We are all in a season of pruning, so that the Master continues to prune and refine our character. Which increases our will desire to look like Christ.

John 15:2
2 Every branch in Me that does not bear fruit He [a]takes away; and every branch that bears fruit He prunes, that it may bear more fruit.

Stages of Pruning

How to Cooperate with Each Stage of Pruning:

1. Stay attached to the Vine- Prioritize communion over productivity. *Apart from Me you can do nothing.* **John 15:5**

   We tend to take each day for granted. We wake with a sense of urgency to fulfill each day. God wants us to not be so focused on what we can accomplish for the day. We must ask ourselves; How closely can I walk with Jesus today?

   We should be Christians that do not pattern our lives by measured output (task or numbers). Our measurement must align with God's word. Can you measure how much time you have spent with God today? Can you measure, your awareness of the Holy Spirit leading, the peace of God, the obedience of God, and his Word?

2. Embracing the Gardener's intent- Pruning is never punishment but preparation for abundance.

For they disciplined us for a brief time based on what seemed good to them, but he does it for our benefit, so that we can share his holiness. 11 No discipline seems enjoyable at the time, but painful. Later on, however, it yields the peaceful fruit of righteousness to those who have been trained by it. **Hebrews 12:10-11**

   We must learn to quiet the soil and let God do the work in us. He knows the exact purpose as to why we need to be cut. He knows the internal struggles, sinful ways, carnal thinking, distant prayers that must be cut away.

   If you will, take one minute to breathe slowly. Get a picture in your mind of a skilled gardener kneeling beside a vine, pruning shears in hand with their eyes full of love, intent on greater harvest. Whisper: Lord, trim what You must; grow what You will. This will cause you to embrace the will for God to prune us.

How to Cooperate with Each Stage of Pruning:

3. Let Scripture interpret the season- Keep a journal of verses He highlights; they often explain what He is cutting away.

As you read God's word, pay attention to any verse that **lights up**, it will be a timely word, it will be something that speaks to you or the state you are in, maybe something that convicts you, or repeatedly catches your eye. Write these verses down and rehearse them, let them get in your spirit.

4. Invite community- Godly mentors can often affirm what needs trimming and remind you of the harvest ahead.

Iron sharpens iron, and one person sharpens another. ***Proverbs 27:17***

5. Pray for sight, not for escape- Father, show me what You are producing through this pruning, and strengthen me to yield.

Pray: Show me Your will, Lord.
- Illuminate the purpose behind each trimming.
- Let Your Spirit whisper the "why" so faith can rise above confusion.
- Reveal the attitudes, attachments, or distractions You are lovingly removing.

Pray: Center my gaze, my attention on Jesus, He is the true Vine.
- Guard me from resentment; grow a spirit of gratitude instead.
- Exchange my urgency for Your timing and my plans for Your perfect strategy.

Pray: Lord, teach me to abide in you while You work.
- Tune my ears to Your daily nudges.
- Give me courage to obey the smallest next step.
- Stir hope for the harvest of righteousness and peace You promise "later on."

Encouragement

If you are feeling the shears right now, remember: **"Every branch that does bear fruit He prunes, so that it will be even more fruitful**." God only trims what He intends to make flourish. The cut may sting, but the grapes that follow will taste all the sweeter—for you and for everyone who will one day feed on your testimony. **It didn't feel good, but it grew me.**

There was a season when everything I leaned on seemed to fall away. God began showing me parts of my life I didn't realize had taken root in pride, and self-reliance.

He started removing relationships that were draining me, opportunities that fed my ego, and routines that looked fruitful, but weren't rooted in Him.

At first, I resisted.

I asked God, why are You taking away things that feel good? Things that are working? Things I built? Things that I thought I needed.

But the more He cut, the more I saw that I had mistaken busy branches for real fruit. It taught me that He wasn't **punishing** me. He was **preparing** me.

During the pruning, I found, peace in silence, strength in surrender, joy in ease and a deeper intimacy with Jesus than I ever had before. Today, I can say that, in was hard being pruned through those tough moments. But I am better because of it.

What's growing in this new season is sweeter appreciation for God, his favor, his strength and His Love. My faith is less about performance and more about presence.

My boundaries are clearer. It's not about who sees me or who I show up for as long as I show up for God. My purpose is more aligned with God's will, not mine.

Looking back, the pruning hurt, but it healed me. It stripped me, but only so something more beautiful could bloom. It took things away, but only so God could give me more of Himself.

So now I can say with full confidence:

Pruning is worth it.

Take courage in that what God cuts away, He will replace it with something better. Know that what He removes, He has the power and strength to redeem them back.

So let him trim and cut off, all of those things that does not look like God, He has created better ahead of you. And the fruit that will follow you, it's not just abundant, it's eternal.

Isaiah 61:3
3 To [a]console those who mourn in Zion, To give them beauty for ashes, the oil of joy for mourning,
The garment of praise for the spirit of heaviness; That they may be called trees of righteousness,
The planting of the Lord, that He may be glorified."

Signs of Pruning Season

Signs You Might Be in a Pruning Season:

→ You feel stripped or stretched but not abandoned.

→ Old patterns no longer satisfy.

→ You sense a call to simplify, surrender, or step back.

→ God's Word feels sharper and more personal.

→ You feel both cut and cared for at the same time.

What to Do in a Pruning Moment

- Stay close to Jesus (abide with God– John 15:4)
- Keep a journal of verses and patterns.
- Pray for insight, not just relief.
- Trust the fruit process. It takes time.
- Praise in the pruning — your worship will fertilize future growth.

Characteristics of a Pruning Season

✓ You feel tested in the same area over again (patience, control, trust).

✓ You've been slowed down, so you can't rely on hustle or talent.

✓ You're seeing uncomfortable truths about your attitude, motives, or temperaments.

✓ You're learning to obey even when you don't see immediate benefits.

✓ God is quiet, but you still feel Him watching over you.

Remember:

A pruning moment is not about loss; it is more about alignment. God is not trying to hurt you...

He is preparing you for abundance.

24

Signs You are in a "Character Refining" Season:

1. Everything Feels Slower Than Expected
God often slows the pace of life when He's working on what's within you more than what's around you. It may feel like you're on pause—but He's preparing you for the next.

"Let perseverance finish its work so that you may be mature and complete, not lacking anything." – **James 1:4**

2. You're Being Confronted with Old Habits or Attitudes
Past struggles or unhealthy patterns resurface, not to shame you, but to prune you.

God is giving you a chance to finally uproot what's been tolerated too long. No longer can you use the excuse, "that's just how I am" or "I am just keeping it real". Trust me, that's the very behavior God wants to change.

"Search me, God, and know my heart; test me and know my anxious thoughts." – **Psalm 139:23**

3. Your Reactions Are Being Tested

You're noticing how you respond to pressure, offense, correction, or disappointment. God uses daily frustrations to reveal hidden motives and sharpen spiritual maturity.

God refines our character by allowing us to experience weakness—so we stop relying on our own strength and start leaning fully on Him.

"A gentle answer turns away wrath, but a harsh word stirs up anger." – **Proverbs 15:1**

Remember:

Let's be clear, this refining season is not a time of ease and comfort. But you will make it through and come out better than ever.

Encouragement

I didn't realize what God was doing at first.

All I knew was things were changing, but not in ways I asked for. I recall when my family and I took the one of the biggest leaps of life and relocated to the state of Georgia. We packed up everything, left our families, friends, jobs, our church, the members, and relationships we built in Delaware.

It was in prayer that God revealed that He was moving us. Now, we had heard it many times, but of course we thought it would be years down the road that God would grow us to the point that we would have to spread out to other areas. This was the biggest pruning in life! Doors were closing. Plans were falling apart. People that we loved and served with stopped calling. And deep inside, I felt like I was being stripped of everything I thought made me strong.

But over time, I began to notice something...

The Fruit Started to Show

I wasn't consumed with comparison like before, I felt content. I didn't need constant affirmation from others, I found confidence in God alone. My husband stopped chasing every opportunity to preach. He found peace in waiting for His direction. I could say "no" without guilt. I could say "yes" to rest. I could worship even when I was hurting.

I started to love differently. I began to teach God's word with more **boldness**. I was no longer focused on how people saw me. The **old me** would have reacted to testing and struggles. But the **pruned me** paused, prayed, and trusted.

Pruning doesn't always show up as blessings dropping from heaven. Sometimes it shows up in the way you carry yourself after the storm. It shows up when you're tempted, but still, you choose God. It shows up when you're tired, and you can still trust God.

And the fruit? It's not just what others see. It's what you feel blooming quietly inside, **peace, maturity, joy and depth**. The fruit of the Spirit is growing where old branches used to hang.

Galatians 5:22–23

"But the fruit of the Spirit is love, joy, peace, patience, kindness, goodness, faithfulness, gentleness, and self-control."

Types of Pruning

How to Identify the Godly Pruning Types:

Surface Trimming

When Jesus first snips away obvious sin or unfruitful habits. This is normally the first cut. You are somewhat prepared. Once saved, you have accepted Christ into your life, to be Lord and Savior. So, you already know that some things will have to be removed to be able to walk in His righteousness.

What It Feels Like

Conviction's Edge – A sudden awareness of a recurring sin or distraction. You begin to since God is wanting you to change.

Holy Spirit Discomfort – The Spirit's gentle but firm nudge, reminding you that something must go. You begin to feel uncomfortable doing the same thing in life.

Fear and Anxiety – Your faith may be tested, and you realize you have been
relying heavy on you own strength rather than God.

Scripture Meditation

If we confess our sins, He is faithful and just to forgive us our sins and to cleanse us from all unrighteousness. **John 1:9**

 Search me, O God, and know my heart; Try me and know my anxieties. 24 And see if there is any wicked way in me and lead me in the way everlasting. **Psalm 139:23-24**

Prayer
Father, shine Your light on anything that dulls my witness for you. I agree with Your findings. I lay it all down to receive cleansing in my soul.
Purify everything in me. Tune my ears to quick conviction and quicker obedience, in Jesus' name. Amen.

Notes

How to Identify the Godly Pruning Types:

Reshaping

God reorders calendars, relationships, and routines so you will not be crowded out by merely good. When God begins to remove people, things, and even relocate you to new areas. This is the reshaping of a life that you thought you knew. God now shows us that He is in control and has more or better for you.

Sometimes, it's not about the people, but more about your **purpose**. People and places can sometimes be a hinderance to you moving further in the things of God. So here is where we allow God to **repurpose** our life, so that the **better** you will show up.

Scripture Meditation

See then that you walk circumspectly, not as fools but as wise, 16 redeeming the time, because the days are evil.
17 Therefore do not be unwise, but understand what the will of the Lord is.
Ephesians 5:15-17

Therefore we also, since we are surrounded by so great a cloud of witnesses, let us lay aside every weight, and the sin which so easily ensnares us, and let us run with endurance the race that is set before us.
Hebrews 12:1

And whatever you do in word or deed, do all in the name of the Lord Jesus, giving thanks to God the Father through Him. **Colossians 3:17**

Prayer

Lord God, prune my environment as boldly as You prune my soul. Show me what to release and where to invest fresh focus. Teach me to number my days and guard my surroundings, so I may gain a heart of wisdom.
Amen.

Notes

How to Identify the Godly Pruning Types:

Heart-Motives
The Spirit exposes pride, people-pleasing, hidden idols, fear, anxiety, etc.

We must know and acknowledge that only God has the ability to **see** and **reveal the true intentions**, desires and motives of a person.

In this pruning, allow God to search **deeply,** the **hidden things**. The things you have not uttered to another person. The things that continue to prevent you from being the best version of you.

Scripture Meditations

Keep your heart with all diligence,
For out of it spring the issues of life. **Proverbs 4:23**

Create in me a clean heart, O God,
And renew a steadfast spirit within me. **Psalm 51:10**

 For do I now persuade men, or God? Or do I seek to please men? For if I still pleased men, I would not be a bondservant of Christ. **Galatians 1:10**

Prayer
Dear Jesus, I give you permission to lay the axe to every root of selfish ambition. Replace pretended humility with the real thing. Let my secret life please You when no one sees, for You alone are my reward. I will trust in your will and way. Amen.

Notes

How to Identify the Godly Pruning Types:

Character-Refining

This is the inner pruning—when God does not just shape your habits, but your heart. This is the **view** that God sees.

If our desire is to be Christ-Like, we must be **refined**. It's when He goes beyond surface behavior and cuts into these: pride, fear, impatience. people-pleasing, insecurity, arrogance, anger, selfishness, bitterness.

These moments often don't involve public changes—they happen in private, where no one sees but God. This must be an invitation to invite God in to do the work, so we become refined by God.

Scripture Meditations

But let patience have its perfect work, that you may be [b]perfect and complete, lacking nothing. **James 1:4**

But we also glory in tribulations, knowing that tribulation produces perseverance; 4 and perseverance, character; and character, hope. 5 Now hope does not disappoint, because the love of God has been poured out in our hearts by the Holy Spirit who was given to us. **Romans 5:3-5**

6 In this you greatly rejoice, though now for a little while, if need be, you have been grieved by various trials, 7 that the genuineness of your faith, being much more precious than gold that perishes, though it is tested by fire, may be found to praise, honor, and glory at the revelation of Jesus Christ. **1 Peter 1:6-7**

Prayer
To My Father and Gardener, I won't waste this storm. Please build up your patience, depth, and unshakeable hope in me, until I look like you Jesus. Keep chiseling away all that does not belong., and while You work, I will keep praising You, Lord. Amen.

Notes

How to Identify the Godly Pruning Types

Mission-Focusing

He may cut even **"fruitful"** branches that aren't part of your specific calling. I like to name it, **a disruption of comfort**. When he leads you out of your comfort zone into unfamiliar territory. Follow Him.

This can be one of the hardest cuts you will ever make. Some cuts you can get an understanding, but these are the ones, where understanding won't come until after the season of it is over (whew!).

It has been by far one of the hardest cuts in my own personal life. This season, it's just you and God. He is grooming your **trust level**.

It's in these moments of weakness and vulnerability you will find yourself relying more heavily on God's grace and strength. You must remember that God has a mission for why he is cutting you. **Surrender** and **let go** of your own plans and **trust God's will** and **timing**.

Scripture Meditations

They were **forbidden by the Holy Spirit** to preach the word in Asia. After they had come to Mysia, they tried to go into Bithynia, but the [b]Spirit **did not permit them**. 8 So passing by Mysia, they came down to Troas. 9 And a vision appeared to Paul in the night. A man of Macedonia stood and pleaded with him, saying, "Come over to Macedonia and help us." 10 Now after he had seen the vision, immediately we sought to go to Macedonia, concluding that the **Lord had called us to preach** the gospel to them.

Acts 16:6-10
Your ears shall hear a word behind you, saying,
"This is the way, walk in it," Whenever you turn to the right hand
Or whenever you turn to the left.- **Isaiah 30:21**

Prayer
Sovereign Lord, narrow my eyes so that my impact widens. Close doors I would never dare shut and usher me through those I would never dare open without You. I trust Your strategy over my own. Where You lead I will follow. I am ok to be uncomfortable in order to grow.
Amen.

Notes

How to Identify the Godly Pruning Types:

Deep Surrender

This is a place of complete and total trust. You have seen what God did in your former cutting seasons. You are better today because of it. Today as you examine your final cut in this season. You learn to release cherished dreams, plans, comfort, reputation, people, your own identity and you discover that **Christ is enough**.

It is an act of faith to be able to place your life, worries and desires into God's hands. But **HE WILL ALWAYS BRING YOU OUT BETTER! (Amen) This process is whereby you are set apart.** To be God's Holy Vessel of Honor.

Scripture Meditations

But what things were gain to me, these I have counted loss for Christ. 8 Yet indeed I also count all things loss for the excellence of the knowledge of Christ Jesus my Lord, for whom I have suffered the loss of all things, and count them as rubbish, that I may gain Christ 9 and be found in Him, not having my own righteousness, which is from the law, but that which is through faith in Christ, the righteousness which is from God by faith; 10 that I may know Him and the power of His resurrection, and the fellowship of His sufferings, being conformed to His death. **Phil 3:7-10**

So likewise, whoever of you does not forsake all that he has cannot be My disciple. - **Luke 14:33**

Though the fig tree may not blossom, nor fruit be on the vines;
Though the labor of the olive may fail, and the fields yield no food;
Though the flock may be cut off from the fold, and there be no herd in the stalls. 18 Yet I will rejoice in the Lord, I will joy in the God of my salvation. 19 The Lord God is my strength. He will make my feet like deer's feet, And He will make me walk on my high hills. **Habak 3:17-19**

Prayer
Abba, even if every earthly vine is stripped bare, make Christ my abundance. My hands and my heart are open; prune what You must. I choose joy in the waiting and worship in the mystery. You are enough—now and forever. Amen.

Notes

Encouragement

Looking back, you must be able to look back and see, what has God cut away in this season. I believe that my life was set up by God to be able to help someone go through the pruning process. There are great benefits in being pruned by God and living a surrender life.

My life has surely seen many trials, tests and struggles. But *one* thing for sure **God has never left my side.** He has been my forever guiding light. He has shown me grace in areas when I thought my life was over. He has favored me and blessed me even when I did not deserve any of it. Looking back and seeing all that God has done and continuing to do in my life. All I can say is "Thank you Lord!"

Yes, there will be continued refining moments, but the **cutting is over.** I really can't imagine what I would look like or what type of believer in Christ I would be if I did not **yield** to God's pruning.

I am the type of person that I want to learn and get it right, so I don't have to repeat it. As a child, I was always the same person. My parents did not have to keep telling me the same thing over and over. If they did, it was because I missed a step or did not fully understand.

I want to be the kind of Christian that yields to God's voice and work. Let me first say, I have made many mistakes in my lifetime. Many as a matter of fact! I know that I am not perfect and will still get some things wrong. But when I made up in my mind to fully live for Christ, I knew that I would surrender over everything to Him for His will and glory. I played and pretended very good for a few years.

Until the Lord, asked me **one** question. Where is your **eternal home**? I knew that in that moment I needed to surrender to God to make heaven my home. Pruning was the best thing I could do for my salvation. Number one, accepting Jesus as Lord, and then being filled with the Holy Spirit.

Pruning, allows you to release the controls, open your heart, free your mind and let God do His creative work in you. As people, we tend to think we know what we need or who we are. But God is the greatest designer, architect, craftsman, planner, builder ever seen.
I want to encourage you today. Please do not resist the pruning.

I've watched God cut things away that I thought I needed to survive. I've felt Him tug at relationships, habits, and attitudes I tried to hold onto. I've sat in the stillness of what felt like an empty garden—wondering if anything good would ever grow again.

But can I tell you something?

It was in those very moments that He was preparing the ground for something greater to grow.

Let God keep His hand on you. Even if it stings. Even if He's silent. Even if you don't understand it yet.

Because I've been there. **It will be worth the cut!**

Journaling Prompts

Taking It All In:
Reflecting on the Pruning

And we know that all things work together for good to those who love God, to those who are the called according to His purpose.
Romans 8:28

Identify the Branch
Which specific habit or sin has surfaced repeatedly in your thoughts or actions?

Describe the Snip
How did God bring it to your attention, was it through Scripture, a friend's word, a circumstance, a teaching?

Anticipate the Fruit
What positive fruit (e.g., integrity, freedom, deeper peace, stronger in your faith) might appear once that habit is removed?

Next Step
What is one immediate act of obedience you can take today to hand over the shears? (confession, accountability partner, deleting an app, closing of a relationship)?

JOURNAL
your
Pruning Journey

_____

_____

_____

_____

_____

_____

_____

_____

_____

_____

_____

_____

_____

_____

_____

_____

_____

_____

_____

JOURNAL
your
Pruning Journey

_____

_____

_____

_____

_____

_____

_____

_____

_____

_____

_____

_____

_____

_____

_____

_____

_____

_____

_____

GROWTH

Taking It All In:
Reflecting on the Pruning

Naming the Growth

- "What fruit is now growing where the cuts once stung?"

- Have you noticed new attitudes, deeper peace, stronger faith, more compassion?

- Are you more focused? More surrendered? More joyful?

- "Because of this pruning, I now walk in _____, and I no longer cling to _____."

Honoring the Process

- "What did God teach me while I waited or wrestled?"

- Was there a truth or promise you clung to?

- Did you learn to trust Him in a new way?
  Example: "In the stillness, I discovered God was _____.
  I learned that I am _____ in Him."

JOURNAL
your
Pruning Journey

_____

_____

_____

_____

_____

_____

_____

_____

_____

_____

_____

_____

_____

_____

_____

_____

_____

_____

_____

Taking It All In:
Reflecting on the Pruning

Recognizing the Refinement

- "What part of my character is more like Jesus now?"

- Is your response to stress different?

- Has your love for others grown deeper?

- What heart change can only be explained by God?
  Example: "I used to respond to _____ with
  _____.
  Now I respond with _____."

Thanksgiving & Celebration

- "Where can I praise God for how far we've come?"

- Write a praise report. Celebrate the beauty from ashes. Even if the full fruit hasn't ripened yet, I will celebrate the budding.
  Example: God, I thank You for pruning me in love. I now see Your hand in
  _____.
  I am still believing You for _____.

JOURNAL
your
Pruning Journey

Encouragement –
For Those Who Made it Through the Pruning

Beloved, you made it.

Through the cutting, the shedding, the stripping—

You remained. You didn't give up. You didn't run.

You stayed rooted in Jesus.

The pruning season wasn't easy.

You may have cried.

You may have questioned.

You may have wanted to quit.

But God was working in the hidden places—

Not to harm you, but to shape you.

Not to break you, but to bless you.

Now, you're not the same.

There's more grace in your walk.

There's more power in your prayer.

There's more fruit on your branch.

You survived the season that was meant to strengthen you.

And what the enemy hoped would make you bitter—

God used to make you better.

Hebrews 12:11
Afterward it yields the peaceable fruit of righteousness to those who have been trained by it.

So hold your head high. This is your fruitful season. This is your testimony season.

This is the **beginning of your harvest.**

Prayer
Seals
It

Prayer Seals the Cutting

Prayer of Thanksgiving

Lord, We praise you for having a precise Hand
Thank You for every holy cut, every quiet removal, every
uncomfortable reshaping.
I see now what I could not see then, You were preparing me for
greater fruit.
Help me hold on to these lessons.
Anchor me in truth when the next pruning season comes.
And let me never forget, that You prune not to harm, but to
grow me into someone who looks more like Jesus.
In full gratitude,
Amen.

Prayer Seals the Cutting

Prayer of Trust

Lord, I Trust Your Hand
Father, I admit this pruning hurts.
I don't always understand what You're cutting away or why
You've chosen this season to do it.
But I trust that Your hand is gentle, and Your plan is perfect.
Where I see loss, help me see love.
Where I see emptiness, help me believe abundance is coming.
Remind me that You prune only to produce greater fruit.
I release my need for control and say:
Have Your way, Gardener of my soul.
In Jesus' name, Amen.

Prayer Seals the Cutting

Prayer of Strength

Lord, "Give Me Grace to Endure"
The cutting feels heavy, and my heart feels weak.
Give me strength to stay rooted in You.
When I am tempted to run from this process,
pull me closer to the Vine.
When I want to give up,
remind me that fruit takes time.
Fill me with Your Spirit—
with patience, faith, and hope—
until this season turns into a harvest.
Amen.

Prayer Seals the Cutting

Prayer of Surrender

Jesus, "I Hand Over the Shears"
Whatever You see in me that does not glorify You, Take it away.
Cut what You must, prune what You will,
and shape me until I look more like You.
Even if it means letting go of my plans,
my comfort, or my pride,
I yield it all.
You are the Vine, and I am only a branch.
Keep me connected to You, even when it hurts.
Amen.

Prayer Seals the Cutting

Prayer of Renewal

Father, "Make Me New Through the Pruning"
I believe this cutting is not the end, but the beginning of something new.
Wash me, heal me, and teach me what I need to learn in this season.
Help me forgive where You ask me to forgive.
Help me release what I cannot hold.
Help me walk humbly and faithfully, trusting Your process.
I declare that this pruning will produce righteousness, peace, and joy.
Amen.

Prayer Seals the Cutting

Prayer of Gratitude

"Thank You for Loving Me Enough to Prune Me"
Thank You, Lord, for caring enough to cut away what I don't need.
Thank You for seeing more potential in me than I see in myself.
Instead of resenting this process,
I choose to praise You in the pruning.
Thank You for the fruit I cannot yet see.
I trust You completely.
Amen.

Prayer Seals the Cutting

10 Daily Pruning Prayers

He prunes every branch that does bear fruit, so that it will be even more fruitful." — John 15:2

Day 1 - The Courage to Be Cut

Prayer: Lord, give me the **courage** to let You cut what doesn't belong. Even if it hurts, I trust Your love more than my comfort.

Scripture - John 15:2
He prunes every branch that does bear fruit, so that it will be even more fruitful.

Day 2: Reveal What Needs to Go

Prayer:
Search my heart, God. Show me the attitudes, habits, or people that no longer align with **Your purpose** for me.

Scripture - Psalm 139:23–24
To console those who mourn in Zion, To give them beauty for ashes, The oil of joy for mourning, The garment of praise for the spirit of heaviness; That they may be called trees of righteousness, The planting of the Lord, that He may be glorified.

Day 3: I Surrender My Plans

Prayer:
Father, I lay down my timeline and my to-do list. Prune my striving and replace it with peace and let me **remain** in Your pace.

Scripture - Proverbs 16:9
A man's heart plans his way, But the Lord directs his steps.

Day 4: Let This Shape Me

Prayer:
God, don't just change my circumstances—change my character. Let this pruning produce the **fruit of Christlikeness**.

Scripture - James 1:2–4
My brethren, count it all joy when you fall into various trials, 3 knowing that the testing of your faith produces [a]patience. 4 But let patience have its perfect work, that you may be [b]perfect and complete, lacking nothing.

Prayer Seals the Cutting
10 Daily Pruning Prayers

He prunes every branch that does bear fruit, so that it will be even more fruitful." — John 15:2

Day 5: **Cut the Fear, Grow My Faith**

Prayer:
Lord, Cut away every root of fear and anxiety. Water my **faith** instead. Teach me to trust You when the path is unclear.

Scripture - Isaiah 41:10
Fear not, for I am with you; Be not dismayed, for I am your God. I will strengthen you, Yes, I will help you, I will uphold you with My righteous right hand.

Day 6: **Refine My Heart, Not Just My Actions**

Prayer:
Father, go **deeper** than my behavior. Refine my motives, my thoughts, and the secret places of my heart.

Scripture - Psalm 51:10
Create in me a clean heart, O God, and renew a steadfast spirit within me.

Day 7: **Patience While I Wait**

Prayer:
Lord, I can't see the fruit yet, but I choose to **WAIT**. Teach me patience while You do the invisible work.

Scripture - Galatians 6:9
9 And let us not grow weary while doing good, for in due season we shall reap if we do not lose heart.

Day 8: **Remove the Bitterness**

Prayer:
God, uproot bitterness from my spirit. **Heal the wounds** that feed it and plant forgiveness in its place.

Scripture - Ephesians 4:31–32
31 Let all bitterness, wrath, anger, clamor, and evil speaking be put away from you, with all malice. 32 And be kind to one another, tenderhearted, forgiving one another, even as God in Christ forgave you.

Prayer Seals the Cutting

10 Daily Pruning Prayers

He prunes every branch that does bear fruit, so that it will be even more fruitful." — John 15:2

Day 9: **I Receive the Peace of Pruning**

Prayer:
Thank You, Lord, that even in cutting, You are careful. Let Your peace fill all empty places you've cleared out **for your glory**.

Scripture - Hebrews 12:11
11 Now no chastening seems to be joyful for the present, but painful; nevertheless, afterward it yields the peaceable fruit of righteousness to those who have been trained by it.

Day 10: **Let the Fruit Remain**

Prayer:
Jesus, may this prune **produce fruit that remains**—fruit that glorifies You, blesses others, and lasts forever.

Scripture - John 15:16
You did not choose Me, but I chose you and appointed you that you should go and bear fruit, and that your fruit should remain, that whatever you ask the Father in My name He may give you.

JOURNAL
your
Pruning Journey

_____

_____

_____

_____

_____

_____

_____

_____

_____

_____

_____

_____

_____

_____

_____

_____

_____

_____

_____

JOURNAL
your
Pruning Journey

_____

_____

_____

_____

_____

_____

_____

_____

_____

_____

_____

_____

_____

_____

_____

_____

_____

_____

JOURNAL
your
Pruning Journey

_____

_____

_____

_____

_____

_____

_____

_____

_____

_____

_____

_____

_____

_____

_____

_____

_____

_____

_____

JOURNAL
your
Pruning Journey

_____

_____

_____

_____

_____

_____

_____

_____

_____

_____

_____

_____

_____

_____

_____

_____

_____

_____

_____

_____

About the Author

Mary H. Blake is an author, life coach, content creator, and the Founder & Chief Editor of MHB Publishing Company. A native of Pennsylvania, Mary now resides in Georgia with her beloved family. She is joyfully married to her purpose partner and the love of her life, Calvin Blake. Together, they have faithfully served in ministry for over 20 years and currently pastor The Worship Center Inc., located in the Atlanta metro area. Mary is the proud mother of two children, Isaiah and Krystal, grandmother to her precious grandson Jayce, and spiritual mother to Sheena. Her heart for family and spiritual growth is evident in everything she does.

Raised alongside nine siblings in a faith-filled household, Mary's upbringing was deeply rooted in church life. Her parents kept her active in youth ministry, igniting her lifelong passion for working with children and writing. Her love for writing began in childhood, when quiet moments became opportunities to craft heartfelt poetry and short stories. That early spark blossomed into a divine calling—to uplift, inspire, and lead others through the written word. Over the years, she has helped lead youth groups, mentor young believers, and encourage women in their spiritual journeys.

When she's not writing or ministering, Mary enjoys quiet reflection and quality time with her family. Her love for God and His people shines through in every chapter she writes—and in every life she touches. Her life is marked by purpose, compassion, and an unwavering commitment to help others grow in faith and discover their God-given identity.

www.ingramcontent.com/pod-product-compliance
Lightning Source LLC
Chambersburg PA
CBHW052212090426
42741CB00010B/2515